T

MW01289232

**A Cosmic Duffer's ™
Companion to**

The Ancient Game of Golf

Cosmic Duffer

™

Sacred Ruminations and
Profane Observations about
Golf and Life

Dan Camilli

1

Dedication

For my beloved wife, Tandy; from whom all good things emanate. And to the cherished memory of my cat, Key West Charlie, who taught me much about courage and the power of love.

Acknowledgements

Special thanks to my first golf partner, Gino T. who had the patience to play with a complete novice. And to my long time golf bud, Norm C. who was often there when I wasn't gazing into the mystery alone.

This work is also dedicated to the memory of Bill Kenney and to Elliot Ernest who taught me about the healing power of caring teachers and to caring teachers everywhere. And to the loving memory of my parents, Dan and Genevieve, and brother, Gus; I lost you all at the turn but have done my best to make you proud of my back nine.

A special shout out and much love to Joan P. who first suggested that I should write a book about golf and philosophy. And to my good friend of lo, these many years, "Steven J."

About the Author

Dan Camilli earned graduate degrees from both Harvard University and the University of Maryland at College Park. He graduated with a B.A., Magna Cum Laude, from the University of Massachusetts at Boston (Boston State College).

Dan studied Eastern philosophy and culture in China, Taiwan and Hong Kong as a Fulbright Distinguished Awards in Teaching Scholarship recipient. He then continued his studies in Japan as a Keizai Koho Fellow; after which he received a grant from the National Endowment for the Humanities to conduct independent research at Harvard's Fairbank Center for East Asian Research and the Reischauer Institute of Japanese Studies in order to develop curriculum for his award winning courses in philosophy, history and world cultures.

Dan lives in Florida with his wife, Tandy, five rescued cats and an ever growing family of putters.

Table of Contents

"Golf is a dark night of the soul in broad daylight."

Anonymous

"He who would attain self knowledge should frequent the links."

Arnold Haultain

Introduction

I am a duffer. I am also a long time student and teacher of philosophy –both East and West. I took up golf at the age of 51, amazingly, at the insistence of my devotedly non athletic wife who wanted some activity that we could share. We purchased starter sets with credit card points and set out to our local muni for lessons. Her infatuation with the game died after a few Saturdays swatting balls hither and yon in the brutal Florida summer sun. But I got the bug. I directly experienced the metaphysical aspects of the game and was immediately entranced; thus I became a **"Cosmic Duffer"**, **always seeking to better understand the spiritual principles underlying the physical and mental aspects of this ancient game; and**

8

constantly striving to better comprehend golf's deeper sub-textual lessons as applied to myself and the world.

I know exactly when I fell in love with golf. It was on the range where I accidently "pured" a seven iron and watched it soar straight and true against the cloudless blue Florida sky. Today, my wife's clubs collect dust in our garage and I, having long since upgraded my bag, play two or more rounds per week.

While this book may be helpful to any golfer of any age it is particularly targeted to men and women like me, who come to golf rather late yet become entranced by its layers of contradictions and meaning...it is an exquisitely simple yet complex game that functions on so many levels; a moving meditation; an 18 hole drama with plots and subplots much like a Shakespearean play. Yet the protagonist, the hero and the villain, are always the same person: you.

Golf is a drama that, at its best, reflects the classical Greek ideal of body, mind and spirit as all are indeed, essential to successful golf. All three are critical elements of golf but many golfers focus exclusively on one or two while either ignoring or unaware of the others.

This is **not** an instruction book. Heavens knows we've got more than enough of those out there already; each golfing guru offering sometimes contradictory strategies to a better game, often resulting in depressed hopes and a still more depressed wallet. By physical I mean the actual physical interactions one has with others and with the equipment and paraphernalia of the game including playing partners, foursomes, starters, rangers, teaching pros, cigars and the like. You know, the stuff that really matters beyond Hogan's swing plane and the Vardon grip.

A Cosmic Duffer believes that golf is a personally transformational kind of moving meditation like Tai Chi Chuan.
And while it is enjoyable as a simple physical activity, there's far more to the picture for the astute observer. One of the most intriguing aspects of the game is that golf can be viewed as a kind of three dimensional, Rorschach test and what one sees and learns depends very much on the conscious awareness of the golfer. **The Cosmic Duffer understands that the game may be approached from the more**

10

mundane ego or, more rewardingly, from the soul.

This book is organized much like the Chinese Classic, Tao Te Ching which consists of 81 brief "Chapters" designed for personal reflection and contemplation. Here you will find 18 "holes" (number 81 reversed!) which, like actual golf holes, are presented as a challenge to your skills and personal awareness. Feel free to "Tee Off" at the first hole or approach the book in "shotgun start" style; opening to any hole and playing it. Another way to approach this book is to permit yourself to attune to whatever topics attract you. Other chapters may draw your attention at another time. Trust your intuitive self to decide what best serves you in the present moment. As the Taoists say:

"When the student is ready, the teacher appears."

If you have read this far I trust that you instinctively know what I'm talking about and have long wanted to discuss these matters but never seem to find a way to do so with anyone at your club. Consider this book our personal 19th hole where we'll just kick back with a cold adult beverage, light a cigar (cigars and pipes are always permitted in this clubhouse!) and reflect upon what we see and do every day on our round in all its sublime and absurd glory.

I suggest that you keep this little book in your golf bag to thumb through while waiting for slow play ahead. Consider each chapter a kind of reflective encounter from which to seek personal meaning; a **Linkster's** *Tao Te Ching.* May it serve as a reminder to slow down, breathe and take in your larger environment-both inner and outer, with fresh eyes thus dissipating your growing anger and frustration over the endless course delays. Who knows, it may just save your round if not your sanity.

What Bagger Vance Didn't Tell You

Golf's Ancient Origins: China, not Scotland.

Say It Isn't So, Lad!

According to Professor Ling Hongling of Lanzhou University, (Smith, P. 2006), the Chinese were playing golf 1,000 years ago.

There is compelling and substantive evidence which points to golf's earliest origins being in China and not the widely believed "home of golf" in Scotland. A museum in Hong Kong holds much of the evidence in the form of a Ming Dynasty (1368-1644) scroll entitled "The Autumn Banquet" which depicts members of the Royal Court swinging what appear to be golf clubs in an attempt to hit a ball into a hole. There is also a reproduction of a Yuan Dynasty (1271-1368) mural which again, shows people engaged in a game that looks much like golf.

The Autumn Banquet" is a pigment on silk scroll painting by Youqui, that clearly shows the Chinese playing Chuiwan ("Hit Ball") as early as 1368 which places them a good 89 years before 1457 when St Andrews Golf Course claims the first recorded mention of golf. The scroll is housed at the Hong Kong Heritage Museum along with a book entitled "Wan Jing" ("Manual of the Ball Game") which, in **1282** became the first known published guide to golf. Consequently, it appears that Scotland's Royal and Ancient Golf Club may well be the "Home of Golf" but the "Royal and (truly) Ancient" origins of the game are more likely to be found in China.

National loyalties aside, it is indeed apparent that golf is an activity shared by people all over the world. It is, truly archetypal to the human experience because it manifests itself in our bodies, minds and spirits. And if the Scots wish to persist in their insistence that they are indeed the creators of the game; well so be it. When dealing with an endeavor as archetypal as golf 'tis often best to let myths persist and not permit facts to get in the way of a good story. Let the Scots stake their claim; and the Chinese, as well, for golf belongs to the ages.

Hole #1: Tea/Tee Ceremony

"The Way can be a guide but not a fixed path."

The Tao Te Ching

While in Japan, I was fortunate enough to participate in a traditional Tea Ceremony in the holy city of Kyoto; "City of 10,000 Temples." The Japanese view the ceremonial preparation and taking of tea as a moving meditation requiring precise movements and special tea-making instruments. The essential aspect of the ceremony occurs when participants sip the bitter frothy green matcha tea and then bite into a sweet biscuit; representing the acceptance of both the bitterness and sweetness of life; just as in golf.

Chanoyu or "Way of Tea" is considered a moving meditation that serves to deepen the awareness of participants and focus on the essentials of life. Golf can also be used to this purpose.

Setting out on a round of golf is an 18 Hole ritual replication of the life journey. And like the Zen Tea Ceremony involves precise movements with special instruments called clubs. Filled with anticipation and trepidation, we boldly go forth hoping for the best and girding ourselves for the worst and knowing full well that we shall, in all likelihood, experience both; just as in life.

And while it is good to set goals, like breaking 80, it's more important still to learn the lessons that the course presents this day. Thus, through awareness, allowing the journey as well as the destination to guide and enlighten us in both golf and life.

The act of creation is Divine. As you set forth from the first tee, ask yourself "What kind of round do I wish to create this day?"

"Upset that you beat me? Of course not.
I love being humiliated in front of my friends."

Hole #2: Tee For Two

"I never found a companion as companionable as solitude."

Henry David Thoreau

Walden

Golf is a game played alone while with others, but for the Cosmic Duffer seeking more than just a "social" round, four is often far too many "others." The best way to reap the full benefits of a round is with but one playing partner. In golf, deuces are wild. Two players move around the course in reasonable time and the best playing partner is like a good waiter/ waitress; there when you need them but invisible when you don't. They provide encouragement and support, applaud your successes and console your defeats but know when to sit in silence- a kind of silence that may give birth to revelation and self discovery. **There is great power in silence**.

Some golfers, like many people, are afraid of being alone. They use group golf to avoid being with themselves. They do not appreciate the difference between lonely and alone. Lonely is when you desire other peoples company but alone is when you are comfortable with yourself. Golf can accommodate either circumstance but has far more to offer the alone than the lonely. Despite their best efforts at group gregariousness, every golfer steps up to the first tee box by themselves. All the nervous energy of trash talk and guffawing subsides as you stand alone on the first tee staring at the long green fairway that begins your days' journey. The nervous chit chat is a physical manifestation of what Eastern thought refers to as leaking "Chi Energy". It is, in this instance, the leakage of anxiety channeled into charged words and actions.

As depicted by the Tarot Card "The Fool" (best illustrated by the Rider-Waite Tarot Card # 0) you set off from the first tee on a great journey into the unknown, full of hope and trepidation. And the journey must begin in silence- the "no-thing" from which emanates the "some-thing". And as the Zen Buddhists say: "You are born and die alone." Ever more so the case on the golf course.

Simply put, foursomes are the single worst idea ever introduced to golf. They are, no doubt, a boon to course operators who can more efficiently and expeditiously herd more bodies through the course and thus on to the 19th hole but they inhibit reflection and turn an essentially introspective activity into a bachelor party. If it's a bachelor party atmosphere you desire perhaps you should take up fishing. Fishing doesn't require the same kind of focus and concentration and one can easily hold up their end of a guffawing confab complete with trash talk without missing a beat with either line or bait. While a raucous and obnoxious fisherman may be disturbing he has little impact on your fishing success or failure but will most definitely affect your ability to putt. Golf is different and frankly commands more attention and respect from its participants. If foursomes were such a great idea don't you think that the professional tours would use them more often?

"Speed bump!"

Hole #3: Golfing Partners and Friends

"Our most intimate friend is not he to whom we may show the worst, but the best of our nature."

Nathaniel Hawthorne

The Ancient Greek philosopher, Aristotle provides us with sound advice regarding the selection of friends – be they for golfing or otherwise. In his classic work, *Nichomachean ethics,* he identifies and defines **three types of friendship based on Utility, Pleasure and Goodness.**

First there is the ***Friendship of Utility*** in which both parties derive some benefit from each other. This is the textbook golf course "business deal" relationship. Aristotle correctly describes this level of friendship as shallow and "easily dissolved ". These friendships are often short lived.

Next, then, comes the ***Friendship of Pleasure***. This relationship is built upon a

23

mutually shared interest or activity such as a passion for golf and is characterized by a feeling of belonging with a person (or group) of like-minded individuals who share your interests. Aristotle points out that this kind of friendship may last only as long as the two share similar passions or interests.

Finally, there is the **Friendship of Goodness** where the two admire each other's virtue and strive to support their further development of character and integrity. This friendship incorporates the other two as the friends will be both useful and provide pleasure to each other but will also, most importantly, express a heartfelt concern for the ethical development of their partner as a human being. Such friendships built on virtue and mutual character development and admiration are rare but are considered by Aristotle to be the best and highest form of human relationship. The Friends of Goodness have similar visions of how their lives and the world should be and strive to help each other grow as human beings of integrity. Alas, meeting a "Friend of Goodness" may seem rather unlikely upon a golf course but one never knows. None the less, 'tis a useful exercise to review all of your relationships both on and off the golf course, and attempt to determine which one of Aristotle's Three Friendships they most appropriately fit.

"Do not have evil-doers for friends, do not have low people for friends: have virtuous people for friends, have for friends the best of men."

Buddha

The Dharmapada

The Cosmic Duffer knows that golf is amongst other things, a moving meditation; a kind of tai chi with clubs. And the way to reap the most from the experience is by one's self or with a carefully selected few others.

Hole # 4: "Discovering Paradise"

"I live in that solitude which is painful in youth, but delicious in the years of maturity."

Albert Einstein

I remember when I was very new to the game and decided to venture out upon the course on my own for the very first time. A teaching pro at my club from whom I was getting some introductory lessons spotted me and said: "Ah! I see that you've discovered paradise." While I wasn't quite sure about the paradise thing at the time, I quickly discovered that golf is an entirely different experience when played alone.

I now play with a partner once a week but also make a point of playing solo at least one additional day. There are many wonderful things to be discovered about this glorious game in the silence and solitude. Being alone is being content with the company of one's self and there are few better places to do so than out in nature on a golf course.

On the physical side, when golfing alone and not being pushed by groups from behind, there is the opportunity to drop an additional ball or two and try that shot again-maybe even with a different club.

On the metaphysical side there is the wonder and splendor of being out in nature without the distraction of human chatter. This permits the mind to cultivate and ruminate about all manner of things. Paying attention to this process permits you to get better acquainted with your entirety.

Early morning, but especially twilight, is the time which the Yaqui Indians refer to as "the crack between the worlds, the door to the unknown" (Casteneda, C. 1968). This is the best time to reap the benefits of solo play as memories, dreams and reflections seem to come more easily. Invite your stream of consciousness to open up and explore all manner of things and you'll find yourself remembering relatives, lovers, dead pets and school experiences. It's also a great place to then clear your head, stop internal dialogue, and effectively examine deeper realities. Indeed, much of this book

28

was written alone on a golf course during this magical time.

When my life becomes chaotic and unclear I will use solo golf as a vehicle to enter my inner world. There is something archetypal, exquisitely primal, about the process of hitting a little white ball with a stick towards a hole in the earth while surrounded by nature. My outer game is a direct reflection of my inner state at any given moment. **When my life is cluttered and chaotic so is my game.** When my life is orderly and under control I find it is then that I am most likely to play my best, and even occasionally enter "the zone" of extraordinarily good golf (for me). **Golf is like life in that it teaches us that little things done well have a cumulative effect (karma) and that the present moment (Eternal NOW) is really all we have; all that is real.** The last hole, good or bad, is but a memory and the next hole is the future. We must be content with and focused upon the **NOW**. We get into trouble when we dwell in the past or the future. Beware of the hole right after a birdie or thinking about an upcoming Par 5 birdie opportunity while imploding on the present Par 3.

29

Golfing alone, especially on foot as this ancient, archetypal game was meant to be played, expands your awareness and puts you more directly in contact with your stream of consciousness - and beyond - to your Higher Self. It amps up and slows down the stream of consciousness on your mind's main screen so you can better examine the flow from thought to thought like so many clouds blowing across a fairway. By then stopping the internal dialogue, you invite Cosmic Consciousness: fully experiencing the Now.

Golf provides us with an opportunity to honestly encounter our Higher Self, should we garner the courage and awareness to seize it. This is most often achieved alone.

"Just how rough is the rough on this course?"

Hole #5: Students and Strategies-
Approaches to Golf and Life

"A man's got to know his limitations"

Golfer Clint Eastwood

Movie: *"Dirty Harry"*

When I first took up the game I was often
told to watch how the old guys play. They
never take unnecessary risks; they lay up,
hit greens; take their bogeys and occasional
pars as well as the treasured birdie
knowing full well that their prudence will
pay dividends when the final scorecard is
tallied. It's not pretty golf and would make
for terribly boring TV but their motto is:
"Scorecards have no video". However, it is
an approach that produces a solid bogey
golfer or better- such as myself.

Younger golfers, in contrast, tend to be risk
takers. They seek the thrill of adventure
and usually find it-in the water or woods.
It's the thrill of high risk/high reward golf
that drives the younger players which is

why they are often obsessed with driving distances.

Driving distance is golf's version of penis size as virtually everybody lies about how long they are.

This is especially true of the younger guys, as they are enamored with the "big stick", and love to drive for show. While the older, more experienced, world weary players knowingly smile at their vain fairway feats while adhering to the old adage that you putt for dough. I, for one, can attest to this strategy, having defeated many a long hitter- guys who out drove me by some 40 or 50 yards no less, with a superior short game. You could build a shopping mall on the space between my drive and theirs yet golf is still as Bobby Jones said: "...about turning four shots into three." And simply putting the ball in the hole first.

The youthful enthusiasm vs. elder experience paradigm of golf is also reflected in life. The young are eager to stretch the boundaries of their experience. Much of their understanding of life is based upon book learning since, alas, they are too young to have experienced much of the "real world". They do not know their own limitations and can only discover them through experience. So when presented with opportunities to engage in real world experiences they tend to push the envelope to the extreme, perhaps subconsciously attempting to discover the boundaries. Fast cars; fast girls and long drives. High risk/ high reward behavior also comes with high penalties. This is the only way in which they can learn and discover who they truly are.

Most of a young person's life is filled with formal schooling and book knowledge. **While essential, book knowledge and formal instruction are not sufficient of themselves for success in either golf or life.**

The older golfer has incorporated the book learning of the games fundamentals but also has the life experience (and scars) to know his limitations and develop a strategy for success; be it on the golf course or the course of life. Indeed, it is a delicate balance developed over time through "hard knocks" that incorporates book learning (basics/ fundamentals) with life experience to produce **Wisdom.** If we focus exclusively on either formal basics (like swing thoughts) or experience we play and live poorly.

It is hard earned wisdom that understands 180 yards on the fairway is better than 280 yards in the woods.

She kept calling the rough the 'pasture' and intentionally hitting the ball into it.

Hole #6: Golf and Cigars

"The Mayan pray by smoking cigars; communicating with the Divine, but also for pleasure."

Iain Gately

Not surprisingly, I began smoking cigars and later, pipes, shortly after I began playing golf. Golf and cigars go together like milk and cookies, rum and coke, Lennon and McCartney. Besides the fact that there are few other places to smoke a cigar in public these days, the golf course also is the ideal venue for a good stogie.

And just like the Mayans, most golfers are smoking both for pleasure and as a form of prayer. For there are no atheists on a golf course. The very process of smoking a cigar is meditative and therapeutic. There is the ritual of cutting, toasting and lighting the stick followed by the gentle, slow first draw.

The experience of cigar or pipe smoking serves to slow one down, to focus on the

37

breath just as in many forms of meditation.

Mild bodied, slow burning cigars are best for the links as more full bodied smokes won't sit well with your stomach when you've got an 8 AM tee time. Forget about the small sizes and leave your Robustos at home. The golf course is for big sticks; Churchills, Toros and double Coronas that stay lit, draw easy and burn even.

While many, including yours truly, find a pipe better suited for reflecting upon the round from the 19th hole, a cigar is, indeed most easily maintained during the ups and downs of play.

Tending to a cigar can calm your angst, soothe your anger and help your game. I was once imploding on the front nine and sparked up a good stogie at the turn. I then played the back nine at par. Best damn nine holes of my life. I still favor that brand smoke on the links to this day.

The golf course is a cathedral, and cigar smoke is the incense carrying prayers to heaven. Sometimes the golf gods even answer them.

"Nice chip shot."

Hole #7: There's No "I" in Golf

" Who everywhere is free from all ties, who neither rejoices nor sorrows if fortune is good or is ill, his is a serene wisdom. "

Krishna to Arjuna

The Bhagavad Gita 2: 57

Much discussion in the sporting world these days involves a phenomenon known as "The Zone". Athletes speak of it in reverential terms with lowered voices as it is a special mental space that one may enter only when the stars are properly aligned and the moon is in the right phase.

Golf, being an individualist game is a very good place from which to examine "The Zone" in order to better understand and appreciate its essential characteristics. Having had brief experiences with "The Zone" myself such as my miracle Par 36 back nine, I cannot explain how I or anyone else gets there but only what it was like.

In The Zone, one enters a kind of Participant-Observer unified consciousness where there is no "I", no "me" there are no swing thoughts, no details, just the pure joy of ball striking where every club you choose is the right one. Every decision you make works. **You've connected with your elemental self and become simple awareness.** That is why it's so dangerous for anyone to point out how well you're playing as it may tear that onionskin layer of consciousness and return you to the mundane dialectical world. When you shift focus to the "I" who is playing well, the magic stops. One literally falls from a state of grace. This is why swing thoughts kill golf games. The state of grace is broken by the re-introduction of the fearful ego- the "I" that's afraid of failure. As Yogi Berra said: *"You can't hit and think at the same time."*

In Buddhist terms, the Zone is connecting with your "No-Self" and visiting Samadhi or bliss-like state of unified consciousness. This is what makes golf an ideal spiritual discipline; an ancient and unique path to transformational consciousness. Zone golf is literally playing "out of your mind." Once you have connected and harmonized with what Eastern Philosophers refer to as the

Tao or Chi energy you attain first- hand experience with the power of creative visualization as you literally can see the flow and path of the ball before the shot is made and then simply execute it. **You then realize that golf is about channeling, harmonizing with, and directing energy through your driver, irons, wedges and putter. Each club has its own, unique energy which is revealed through proper tempo.**

Different people respond to the zone experience in different ways based upon their respective levels of consciousness. Golfers with less awareness may just shrug it off as "a stretch of playing well" while more aware players will marvel at the experience and express silent gratitude. However, like other meditative forms, a golf zone experience can lead to a kind of attachment as the golfer goes out each round hoping to replicate this truly unique experience. This in turn can become an obstacle in itself as the golfer is now focusing on the past and not the present moment and thus develops an attachment to a particular past experience. **This attachment to desire generates what is called a "Forcing Current" which will inevitably undermine his or her strained**

**and stress filled efforts to repeat the
experience instead of living in the Now.**
An essential precept of Eastern thought is
that **one must hold on loosely to desires
and do what must be done without
concern for results.** It is the obsession
with a pre-determined outcome that
induces failure-as in *"I MUST make this
putt! "*

*The Cosmic Duffer is aware of his/her
state of mind and learns to focus
entirely on the simple act of making
shots without concern for its
consequence.* **The entire golf experience
then becomes a mirror upon the self and
an intimate examination of one's
consciousness. Consequently the Cosmic
Duffer encounters not only the course
but him/ herself.**

**The only Zen you will find on the golf
course is the Zen you bring with you.**

"I'd use the nine-iron, but I'm just passing through."

Hole #8: Golf and Karma -"The Philosophers Walk"

"Golf is a physiological, psychological and moral fight with yourself"

Arnold Haultain

In the holy city of Kyoto, Japan there is a pedestrian path along a cherry tree lined canal known as "The Philosopher's Walk". While this walk may take as little as a half hour, it passes by numerous temples and shrines where one may stop to meditate and reflect. The process of walking, reflecting and stopping at a temple to examine one's life is much like that practiced by a golfer.

Each hole is a kind of temple of the soul; testing the mettle of all who pass by; challenging the golfer to go deeper into their game and themselves.

Golf is a reflection of one's state of mind at any given moment. When my life is cluttered with chaos, so is my game. When my inner life is in order I play well and may enter "The Zone"- a place of blissful unity between the physical, mental and spiritual. Golf is a meditation, a moving meditation like Tai Chi or Chi Kung. And just like all meditation, the moment that you think "I've got it! "; you don't.

Improvement in golf, as in life, involves cleaning up karma. Past transgressions like slices, hooks, skulls and chunks must be addressed, resolved and forgotten in order to work towards your **Dharma** (true calling) as a pure golfer as the universe intended. Your golf game is like owning an old car; when you fix one thing, another breaks down.

Golf is a Philosopher's Walk available to anyone with the awareness and will to undertake it. Enlightenment is an egalitarian experience; available to all with the courage to pursue an honest encounter with themselves. One must struggle mightily in order to clean up their personal golf karma and return to what **Bagger Vance calls** *"your Authentic Swing."*

Hole #9: The Power of Visualization and the Subconscious

"You are what you think. All that you are arises from your thoughts. With your thoughts you make your world."

The Dhammapada

According to Perennial Wisdom; a collection of universal truths regarding the nature of consciousness and humanity acquired by ancient Eastern and Western civilizations, thoughts are things-physical entities. What we think, attracts material reality and thus becomes what is. Our minds are image machines and we "think" first in pictures. After which our brains translate the images into words.

Try this little experiment: Close your eyes and think or have a friend say the words "Tree", "Pond", "Frog". Did you see a mental picture of each item? Most people do.

"An old pond.

A frog jumps in.

Splash."

Classic Haiku by Matsuo Basho (Japanese Poet, 1644-1694)

And while our rational minds may have difficulty with this concept, we have all experienced instances when what we were thinking became so; especially when we are blurting things out as affirmations. This phenomenon is often displayed on the golf course. Like most golfers, I have had days when the frustration builds and I start blurting out comments like, "I just can't putt today." Or "Nothing's working for me on this round." And that is precisely what occurs because you are feeding energy to negative thought patterns, karmically stored in the Akashic Records which, according to the Perennial Wisdom, contains all karmic patterns for all incarnated beings.

Thoughts attract material reality, and negativity attracts negativity; the subconscious has no sense of humor.

What you state is what shall become manifest.

The subconscious also doesn't comprehend the negative tense –as in "don't hit the ball into the water hazard". You have probably tried this little experiment yourself and know full well what results; splash! Its' much better understood when we say to ourselves "I'm going to land this ball right on the green." Or better yet, leave "I" out of it. Indeed part of my pre-shot routine when hitting a Par 3 tee shot or an approach shot is to quietly say to myself when addressing the ball: "See you on the green."

I used to play with a partner who constantly belittled his own game as a kind of defense mechanism. A way to put himself down before anyone else did so. He would always announce that he was going to hit this shot into the woods or the waste area etc. with remarkably consistent results. Something akin to Babe Ruth's legendary called shot home run. This kind of negative thinking; even in jest, is contagious much like seeing your partner slice a tee shot into the water hazard before your turn.

After repeatedly failed attempts to enlighten him to the nature of the subconscious and the power of visual imagery, I had to stop playing with him. His level of consciousness was too destructive to himself and to others.

You must erase the mind of these negative images and replace them with positive ones. That is the true definition of mental toughness; to view these negative mental pictures like clouds floating across the sky of your mind; being blown away and replaced by positive images.

Words do indeed have power.

Words stimulate mental pictures both good and bad. Ever have a good round going until someone pointed out how good you were playing? Something like "Wow, Joe, you're really playing lights out today!" Then things come apart. The spiritual reason is that Joe is now self conscious of his "lights out" play and mentally separates the "I" (ego) with doubts from the unified higher consciousness which is simply performing as "expected". Instead of staying in union with spirit and body, Joe's mind now starts to think about how well "HE" is doing thus not being completely in the moment- the Eternal Now.

That which unites is holy; that which separates is profane.

"Zone Golf" is the manifestation of a perfectly integrated and delicate union between body, mind and spirit. The Cosmic Duffer knows it is a unified field energy which can move mountains and jar thirty foot putts.

We have all had rounds or at least holes, where we could clearly visualize what we needed to do-literally see it before it happened and make it so. This remarkable experience is made all the more so by its seeming ease. Visualizing and actualizing become almost effortless when properly focused. This is what many mistakenly refer to as mental toughness which implies great exertion when in fact it is a natural state of grace; of unity between the spiritual, mental and physical. **A state of grace commonly referred to as "The Zone" is a delicate balancing act in which mundane mental constructs such as "I" are integrated with body, mind and spirit as one becomes an empty vessel filled by the Higher Will which will effortlessly produce desired results.** Being in that state is not especially difficult but getting and staying there is the challenge. Paradoxically we often try too hard to play with ease.

Success in golf, as in life, is achieved by trying hard not to try too hard. This is why we are most accurate when we don't swing from our heels but establish a rhythmic tempo; effortless power vs. powerless effort.

"The peculiar thing about this game....is the more you fight it, the more it eludes you. Everything contains its opposite. By trying to make something magical happen, you create the opposite effect-you drive the magic away. When you worry about finding the way, you lose the path...a little less is a lot more."

"Opti the Mystic" aka James Dodson's father

Final Rounds

"Ever tried the Auto-Putter?"

Hole #10: The Proof Is In the Putting

"Thirty spokes meet in the hub. Where the wheel isn't is where it's useful.

Hollowed out, clay makes a pot. Where the pot's not is where it's useful.

Cut doors and windows to make a room. Where the room isn't, there's room for you.

So the profit in what is, is in the use of what isn't. "

Lao Tzu

Tao Te Ching, Chapter 11

Where there is empty space is useful, as in the emptiness of the golf cup. Putting the ball into the cup is the simple (or not so simple) act which constitutes scoring in golf and is thus, the most "useful" element of the game. No one has ever had a good round without putting well. It is the single most important and most subjective aspect of the game. There is simply no one correct way to putt or a single best putter club.

55

Men tend to collect putters like women collect shoes. Endlessly and often futilely searching for the one that listens to them, the one with the magic in it. They nose around golf shops and used club bins handling, examining and testing putters like Harry Potter shopping for a wand. And a magic wand it truly is as the instrument that initiates ball to cup; yang to yin; Shiva to Shakti. Filling the empty vessel and inhabiting its usefulness.

Just as putting is the most subjective aspect of the game, **putters contain different states of consciousness and energy.** Each one presents a different perspective and possesses a different vibration towards accomplishing the same task; holing the ball. This is what attracts "putter hos," like myself, to collecting more putters than I could possibly use. Indeed, I own more than a few that have never even been on a golf course. I enjoy unifying with their unique energy by putting on my office carpet.

There are elegant and refined blade putters, staid and stolid mallets and fantastical futuristic contraptions that look like starships or cattle brands all designed with the same purpose. It is in the area of putters where we most clearly see the multiple levels of consciousness at work in golf; the physical, aesthetic and the metaphysical.

It is quite common for golfers to have several, if not dozens of putters cluttering their closets and garages. Log onto eBay and enter the search word "Putter" and literally thousands of flat sticks that have lost their MoJo for the present owner are up for bid. (35,405 last I checked!)

It should then come as no surprise that many golfers give names to their putters and develop a most intimate relationship with their favorite flat stick. I will not speak too personally about my putter except to say that putting is the very best aspect of my game. I rarely have a round where I don't hole one or more 25 foot plus putts or at least seriously scare the hole. As an older Cosmic Duffer, I am not blessed with great distance off the tee. Consequently, I must defeat big ball strikers with an effective short game and on the green by demonstrating Bobby Jones definition of golf –*turning four strokes into three.*

There are essentially two kinds of putter personalities; there's the "technical" putter and the "feel" putter. The technical putter scrutinizes every blade of grass before rolling his rock. He must deliberate on every swale, real or imagined, from every angle before finally addressing his ball and making a measured stroke. His head is filled with either" in-out-in open gate" or "straight back straight through" stroke thoughts. I find that few of these guys are consistently solid putters. The reason is that they simply over think the stroke and let their mind interfere with the natural life energy (Chi) between the hole and the ball.

In the words of Andrew Lang: ***"He uses statistics as a drunken man uses a lamppost- for support rather than illumination."***

In contrast, the "feel" putter rather casually sizes up her putt, often from only one side, sees her line and goes for it. And while it is true that what you feel may not be real, it is far more important to be confident about your line then it is to be right since a confident swing at the correct speed will often at least leave you with a good lag and easy two putt.

The Cosmic Duffer realizes that what he is attempting to do with his putter is call

forth the feminine energy of the hole (Yin) so that she will attract the masculine energy of the ball (Yang) in cosmic conjugal bliss, consummated by the joyous rattle as the ball tumbles home into Shakti's waiting arms (or opened legs as the case may be).

The best approach therefore in my experience has been to **"See it, roll it and hole it."** Just attune to the energy and visualize the cup sucking up the ball like a bee attracted to a flower. This will usually reveal the line to you. Then address the ball and while looking at the hole take 2 or 3 practice strokes so that your subconscious can determine the correct speed. Address the ball, line up your putter and let it go. Be prepared to hole some remarkable putts. A positive internal tempo may be attained by thinking "Yin-Yang, Yin-Yang" while making your putting strokes. Yin = backswing, Yang = forward stroke.

As with all things golf, your experience may differ. 🙂

"You an obsessive golfer? ... naaaah."

Hole #11: Developing a Pre-Shot Routine

"Distracted from distraction by distraction"

T.S. Eliot

A pre-shot routine is a kind of deliberate distraction designed to distract us from distractions and, most importantly, trigger the process of manifestation.

All golfers seem to agree that developing a pre-shot routine is essential to improving ones game and all professional players have distinct pre-shot routines. While you might copy some aspects of a tour pros routine *it is imperative that you develop one that is uniquely your own.*

The pre-shot routine is designed to focus mind, body and spirit and attune them to the task at hand.

It must be neither forced nor contrived but should serve as a "trigger" mechanism for calling your conscious, subconscious and higher self to attend,

in unison, to the task at hand- to the Now moment.

Most routines start behind the ball; **visualizing** the desired shot followed by a few practice swings in order to connect body-muscle memory to the task. This is accomplished by first softening your focus by relaxing your gaze and then refocusing. In Michael Murphy's classic work "*Golf in the Kingdom*", mystical Scot golf pro, Shivas Irons puts it best when he says: ***"Make the world an Impressionist painting. Then turn yer eyes to a telescope."***

Then comes **"stepping into"** the shot, literally "stepping into" the visualized energy field, by addressing and aiming the ball. This is sometimes followed by a couple more practice swings in order to further inform muscle-memory of the task at hand, and **then the actual shot itself.**

What is actually taking place here is a kind of Kabuki dance which represents the ***Archetypal, Formative Creative and Material Planes*** of reality as described by Plato and other philosophers both East and West.

The visualization aspect taps into the **Archetypal Plane** where all possible golf shots exist, the home of what Steven Pressfield's character ***Bagger Vance refers to as your "Authentic Swing."*** The **Creative Plane** then selects the desired shot; the **Formative Plane** then draws that shot into specific form to meet the needs at hand - one particular type of shot while your practice swings assist the selected shot in manifesting itself into the **Material Plane**.

Check your Pre-Shot Routine to insure that it includes all four of these elements in order to produce successful results. Once you are certain that all four elements are accounted for you should, paradoxically, **forget all of this and allow your higher self to simply conduct the process**.

A Pre-Shot routine is, then, a kind of ritual performed before each and every shot which calls forth the cosmological principles of **Perennial Wisdom**- the collective knowledge of the ages – in manifesting your desired reality.

Visualize, Harmonize, Realize.

Hole #12: Swing Thoughts and Instruction

Junnah: "Anything else?"

Bagger Vance: "Just bash the living shit out of it"

Steven Pressfield, *The Legend of Bagger Vance*

While instruction of some kind, be it personal, video or print is essential to improvement, one can indeed, also suffer from "paralysis from analysis"-literally over analyzing your swing to the point where you are no longer simply hitting the ball. This condition is often referred to as having "swing thoughts." Ironically the best swing thoughts are thought when not swinging as they interfere with the body-mind-spirit unity essential to an effective swing.

Swing thoughts introduce the unwanted company of the ego into your swing and disrupt the natural flow which results from a unification of body-mind and spirit.

This is why, perhaps subconsciously, a solid shot is sometimes referred to as **"Puring" one; it is the result of a pure and true body-mind-spirit union during which you <u>"STAYED CONNECTED."</u>**

Hole #13: Technical Players and Feel Players

"Everything that can be counted does not necessarily count; everything that counts cannot necessarily be counted."

Albert Einstein

There are said to be two kinds of players: Technical Players who attempt to approach the game in a scientific/ analytical manner focusing on issues such as swing plane and the like.

And then there are also "Feel Players" who prefer to approach the game in a less technical fashion-emphasizing and trusting their innate" athletic instincts" in making the correct shot. For example, a feel player's approach to putting is "see it, roll it; hole it" as discussed earlier.

The reality is that the technical and the feel approach are but two sides of the same cosmic coin. There's a science to the art and an art to the science. But science is not art and art is not a science. (Didn't mean to go all Dr. Seuss on you there.) The science approach represents the Yang or male projective energy as we attempt to apply our rational, analytical left brain to golf while our artistic right brain side draws us to be more intuitive players represented by the feminine receptive energy of Yin.

Technical golfers play the game while feel golfers let the game play them.

As is so often the case when we subdivide reality, this is something of a false dichotomy since both technical and instinctual knowledge are essential aspects of effective golf. The trick is to acquire the skills of **both** approaches and then **FORGET** them on the conscious level so that you can enter the **NOW** moment and effectively hit the shot at hand.

Hole #14: Tour Pros and the Greek Gods

"We are not human beings having a spiritual experience; we are spiritual beings having a human experience."

Pierre Teilhard de Chardin

Many golfers of every skill level tend to admire the Tour Pros, who seem to make the game look so easy. For unlike, we, mere mortals, the tour pros consider par a bad score and regularly shoot in the sixties. Their sometimes incredible performances on the biggest stage lead many a duffer, Cosmic or otherwise, to believe that these people have tamed the golf gods and have somehow forced them to submit to their will - at least on some Sundays.

Tour pros are sometimes viewed by the public in much the same manner that the ancient Greeks viewed their thespians or stage actors- namely as people with extraordinary abilities to harness energies and powers unattainable by most humans; capable of manifesting a literal channeling of the Golf Gods upon the earth. The Greek thespians had the ability to transform themselves into many different characters and the Tour Pro seems, at least at times, to have harnessed supernatural powers to make a difficult game look easy. As such they are believed then to be part of a small elite sanctum of souls who share carefully guarded secrets about the "inner game".

Alas, while the duffer may hang on every word from a Nicklaus, Woods or McIlroy, they will mostly discover that this cloistered cabal speaks to the public only in common place generalities but are often suspected to speak to each other about the inner mysteries of the game.

"I made the putts today" or "I hit the fairways and greens" is typical post round interview fare for the commoners as it seems undeniable to some that these players also tap into some deeper realm and often can take their games to what appears like super human levels.

To reveal the true secrets of the inner golf sanctum to the laity would be akin to "casting pearls before swine" as many have not the consciousness to process this wisdom-much less apply it. This is not to suggest that all tour pros are consciously aware of this "high church of golf" any more than Shakespeare was necessarily conscious of all the levels of narratives and subtexts presented in his plays. However, it's also interesting to note that an increasingly large number of these tour pros are employing sports psychologists in order to better assist them with this "intangible", yet essential component of the game. This may be considered a small yet significant example of the continuing evolution of our individual and collective consciousness - a recognition that we are more than our physical selves.

"A change of consciousness is the major fact of the next evolutionary transformation,
and the consciousness itself, by its own mutation,
will impose and effect any necessary mutation of the body."

Sri Aurobindo Ghose

Hole #15: "Tee It Forward" vs. Testosterone

"Only two things are infinite, the universe and human stupidity, and I'm not sure about the universe"

Albert Einstein

One of the most discouraging experiences encountered on a golf course is a group in front of you playing military golf ("left, right, left") from what is obviously the wrong tee box.

This phenomenon tends to be more common among two kinds of golfers: the young bucks in their twenties who simply must prove to everyone (especially their bored girlfriend doing her nails in the cart) that they are indeed, the next Tiger or Phil; and sadly, the old timers who are experiencing golf's version of a mid-life crisis. Instead of the red convertible and the daughter-aged blond mistress, these codgers are adding a good hour or so to everyone's round by hitting from the "Pro Tees." This is the aging linkster's version of

Viagra and the only ones getting a "rise" out of it are the poor devils stuck behind them.

Search any on-line golf discussion board these days and you will find their smug posts defending their God –given right to never break 100 while slowing play for all who may be so unfortunate to follow them.

They take especial umbrage at the recent PGA and USGA initiative called **"Tee It Forward"** which has the audacity to actually apply reason and common sense to what course length a golfer should play.

TEE IT FORWARD

The genius behind the "Tee It Forward" concept is equipment manufacturer Barney Adams of Adams Golf fame. And like many strokes of genius, it is remarkably simple. You would not expect Little League baseball players to hit home runs in a park with major league dimensions, so neither should amateur golfers be expected to make par on Tour Professional length courses. Teeing off from the appropriate distance permits amateurs to use the same short irons and wedges as the pros on their approach shots and actually have a

76

legitimate shot at Greens in Regulation
(G.I.R.).

This chart, courtesy of the PGA and the
USGA, is a guide to help golfers align their
average driving distance with the course
length best suited to their actual (not
imagined) abilities.

Driver Distance**	Recommended 18-Hole Yardages**
275	6,700-6,900
250	6,200-6,400
225	5,800-6,000
200	5,200-5,400
175	4,400-4,600
150	3,500-3,700
125	2,800-3,000

**Courtesy of PGA website:
http://www.pga.com/pga-and-usga-step-new-sets-tees-in-nationwide-tee-it-forward-initiative

The golf stats gurus at Trackman, (http://blog.trackmangolf.com/performance-of-the-average-male-amateur/) have assessed over 10,000 golfers of all abilities world-wide, and provide additional hard data which serves to further support the "Tee It Forward" concept.

According to Trackman:

"The Average Male Amateur (AMA) has an average club speed of 93.4 mph and an average total distance of 214 yards."

Yep....that's driving it a whopping 214 YARDS, Sparky!!   Reality Check for "Testosterone Tony"!

And let's not forget that this is the **AVERAGE** and that a full **HALF** of us amateurs perform at a level considerably **BELOW** this number!

According to the PGA**,** *"The 6,700-yard course that many amateur golfers play today is proportionally equivalent to a PGA Tour player competing on a course measuring 8,100 yards -- 700 yards or more longer than a typical PGA Tour layout."*

Consequently, we can readily deduce that it is highly unlikely that **ANY** weekend warrior should be playing a course longer than approximately 6,000 yards.

Hole #16: Golf is a Walking Game

"Golf is a lot of walking, broken up by disappointment and bad arithmetic"

Anonymous

Before there was the golf cart, there was golf. The game was originally designed to be played on foot.

Alas, today in the United States, there are increasingly fewer courses that permit walking, thanks in good part to the Darwinian "survival of the fittest" brutality of golf course economics. For it is far more cost effective to swiftly move customers through the course and on to the 19th Hole Lounge by motorized means than afoot. But, besides good exercise, something of great value is also lost in this Faustian Bargain.

Today there are a growing number of golfers who have never experienced the game as played on foot-as it was meant to be played-and consequently have never had an opportunity to encounter and savor much of what makes the game so special. It is a difference much akin to driving vs. hiking through the giant redwoods of northern California. Driving may be more "efficient" but you certainly miss a lot!

According to Perennial Wisdom; the universal wisdom and teachings of Eastern and Western Thought, all living things are made up of **a universal life energy or life force.** In traditional Chinese it is called **"Chi,"** in Indian Hinduism it is **"Prana,"** and in Ancient Greece it was called **"Pneuma**." Since all things contain the life force, including ourselves we are literally bathing in "Chi" energy when we are out in nature. Chinese Taoists believe that these walks in nature restore and rejuvenate us because we are "reconnected", "recharged" and nourished by the earth's chi energy.

Consider how you feel after a long walk on the beach or in the mountains vs. a long trudge through a shopping mall. The former serves to refresh, relax and rejuvenate while the latter enervates us as we are not engaged with the nourishing chi energy of the natural world when prowling the food court. This same kind of energy replenishment through nature can be experienced by walking the golf course.

An often overlooked energy center of the body is located in the soles of the feet. According to Eastern thought, it is through the foot soles pathways called "Nadis" that Chi energy is transmitted to the first energy center or Chakra located at the tailbone called the Muladhara Chakra .

This is why people enjoy walking barefoot in nature as they can sense this energy rush more completely resulting in a pleasurable experience. Engaging with Chi in this manner tends to relax us, slow us down, helps us breathe more deeply from the belly drawing the energy up into the lower "dan t'ian or power center-located just below the belly button, leading to greater vitality and permitting us to see our surroundings with greater clarity and insight. The Chi then proceeds to the middle dan t'ian located at the heart center which improves respiration and finally on to the upper dan t'ian or "Third Eye", located at the mid forehead just above the eyebrows, associated with the pineal gland and spiritual or "cosmic consciousness".

One direct result of this process as it pertains to golf is that walkers often have better "tempo" than cart players since they are more directly connected to the earth's chi energy and stride toward their next shot while enveloped in this "elixir field." Indeed, many cosmic experiences occurring on golf courses are attributable metaphysically to the flow of Chi energy through the foot Nadis and upward through the three primary dan t'ians and ultimately all seven major Chakras.

This is a rather elaborate Eastern metaphysical explanation which basically translates as **"Walking the golf course is good for you."** Just sayin'.

The serenity and power inherent in walking the golf course was never more apparent to me than when I teed it up in Dublin, Ireland where golf carts are extremely rare, used most often only by the seriously disabled; so virtually everyone walks the course. Because of the absence of carts, I was surrounded by a rich deep "roaring silence" as vivid as the lush fairways and greens of the course itself. Unlike on many American cart-based courses, there was nary a single loudmouth player as no golfer dared raise his voice and disrupt the sacred silence and moving meditation of the parishioners attending the "High Church" of golf.

"Let me know if I am
distracting you."

Hole #17: "Pairing Up" - Golfers and Other Strangers

"Two's company, three's a crowd"

American Proverb

When my wife and I go to a restaurant the manager doesn't try to pair us up with another couple for dinner. And golf is a far more intimate exercise than dining.

As a Cosmic Duffer, I find one of the more disturbing policies at many courses these days is to "pair up" total strangers for a round of golf. While some may look upon this practice as an "opportunity to meet new friends" and the like; it seems more than a little intrusive to do so without the consent of all parties For when you view a round of golf as does the Cosmic Duffer –as a potentially transcendent and transformative experience, being abruptly paired with a total stranger is much akin to inviting your mother-in-law to live with you. With very rare exceptions, a bad idea.....a very bad idea.

Indeed golf courses are behaving in a remarkably short sighted fashion when they insist on this "pairing up" practice as while it may be more lucrative in the short term to "pack them in", they are risking future patronage and general support for the game by golfers far more likely to have a bad experience on their course.

The Cosmic Duffer- friendly course permits golfers to play in whatever manner they see fit from singleton to foursome (although some courses, reprehensibly permit five playing partners –and I've seen as many as EIGHT!!).

Which brings us to the matter of playing partners. I have discovered through bitter experience that they come in three forms: Good, Bad and Ugly.

First, in keeping with the generally optimistic tenor of this book, we begin with the good.

A good partner has many of the qualities of a good spouse: they are kind, compassionate, empathetic, and know when to compliment, encourage and yes, criticize. They may or may not perceive of the game as you do but they are engaging, supportive companions with whom you can share, vent and commiserate at day's end. They feel no need to fill sacred silent space with idle banter and are there when you need them, and are not when you don't. These quality partners are few and far between and should be cherished as the treasures that they, indeed are. You actually look forward to a 19th Hole beer with them after the round.

The bad partner not only displays behavior counter to that describing a good partner but also fails to respect personal space and boundaries both physical and psychic. They are constantly filling your sacred silence with disruptive energy – chasing away any potential encounters with the angels of our better nature.

The ugly partner not only engages in similar practices as the bad partner but insists on "helping" you with your golf game as well. Giving you unsolicited "tips"; "helping" you read greens without being asked and the like. He often also engages in shouting out advice to other groups along the way; steps on your line; and doesn't provide ample psychic or physical space to play your ball. All while, himself, playing like crap and losing balls with such reckless abandon that in the words of an anonymous caddie in Kilkenny, Ireland:

"Were the ball wrapped in bacon, Lassie herself, would not be able to find it."

Play this game long enough and you will likely encounter all three of these archetypal personalities; alas, a true cross section sample of humanity which I suppose in itself has some redeeming karmic value.

"This might be our last round of the year."

Hole #18: Breaking "80" - On Making Haste Slowly

"It's a wise man who knows the seasons"
Lao Tzu

I had shot a splendid "38" on the front nine, parred #10 and was abruptly chased off the course by a blustery storm. We had been playing this pricey course on a one-time discount deal which was only valid for that day. Intoxicated by visions of breaking "80", I decided to hang around the rain-soaked golf course after my more sensible playing partner had left; hoping for a small hole in the storm that might permit me to finish the round. This, in spite of being shown <u>three</u> different real- time weather radar maps of increasingly worsening conditions!

Well, such a hole in the torrential rains did indeed appear, albeit briefly, and I quickly decided to go get my cart back and continue playing. When I went to do so, there was a cart shed worker just about to take it away and I explained to him what I wanted to do.

He told me that the Club Pro had checked the forecast and seen only worsening conditions. In fact, the Pro had been told that there was a good chance of hurricane-like conditions, and instructed the grounds crew to go out and collect the pins from all the holes. He decided to evacuate the course and shut down for the day.

Perhaps because he noticed my partner's handicap flag on our cart or just out of kindness-having seen my crestfallen expression - the course attendant offered to give me a lift back to my car. As he did so, I thanked him for talking some common sense into an unrepentant golf addict who might well have risked serious harm in hot pursuit of his long held and in this case, potentially dangerous obsession; and for providing me with a valuable lesson about the destructive nature of uncontrolled desires. The quest to break "80" would have to wait another day. Alas, stymied by the forces of common sense.

"Nothing brings suffering as does the untamed, uncontrolled, unattended and unrestrained heart full of desires. That heart brings only suffering"

Buddha
The Anguttara Nikaya

The 19th Hole: "It's Just Golf"

"When we practice gratefulness there is a sense of respect toward others"

His Holiness the XIV Dalai Lama

I hit what the Irish call a "Mother-in-Law" shot ("she looked good leaving") off the tee on a 140 yard par 3 that plunked into the left bunker; thus short-siding myself on the beach. As I angrily stomped my way down from the elevated tee box I was met by a groundskeeper passing by in a cart.

"How you doing?" he politely inquired.

To which I grumbled "Not so good. I hit the damn bunker!"

"It's just golf", he calmly replied.

"Wanna change places?" he asked as his cart trundled off; attending to the seemingly endless landscaping task that is a golf course.

On this day, that groundskeeper served as an angel delivering an important message of which Cosmic Duffers often need to be reminded: **Playing golf is a blessing**. Something to be enjoyed and savored in all its aspects. Being out in nature; fresh air; amongst wildlife and playing this endlessly fascinating game is truly a gift; a privilege for which we must constantly express gratitude regardless of what our scorecard looks like on any given day.

Golf, much like life; is unpredictable, exhilarating and at times unfair.

In golf, as in life, it's important to savor and express gratitude for the journey as well as the destination.

Final Swing Thoughts:

"For the gods love to thwart whatever is greater than the rest. They do not suffer pride in anyone but themselves."

Herodotus

There is a sweet futility to this seductive and addictive game of golf - a kind of Sisyphean fatalism. For one can never truly conquer golf any more than Sisyphus could successfully roll that boulder up the hill in Ancient Greek mythology.   However there is a certain satisfaction, a redemption, if you will, to be found in perseverance; in fighting the good fight against all odds. And much to be learned about oneself and others in the process.

When golfers kiddingly ask me and my partner, "Who's going to win today? ", I always reply, "the course." For the course is the teacher and the golfers will learn what they may this day.

Da Vinci said *"A painter should begin every canvas with a wash of black, because all things in nature are dark except where exposed by the light."*

On the golf course, the back wash may be green but the conscious golfer, **the Cosmic Duffer, is always employing it as a tool to shed further light upon him/herself.**

"Be a lamp unto yourself."

Buddha

Fairways and Greens, Cosmic Duffer!

Visit us at **cosmicduffer.com**

Select Bibliography

Aristotle, & Sachs, J. (2002). *Nicomachean ethics*. Newbury, MA: Focus Pub. / R. Pullins

Bowler, P. (2001) *The Cosmic Laws of Golf*. NY, NY: Berkley Publishing Group

Casteneda, C. (1968) *The Teachings of Don Juan; A Yaqui Way of Knowledge*. Berkeley, CA. University of California Press

Chardin, P. (1977). *The Phenomenon of Man* (Revised ed.). London: Fount Paperbacks

Chopra, D. (2003) *Golf for Enlightenment*. NY, NY: Harmony Books

Clint Eastwood, Dirty Harry [Motion picture]. (2008). Distributed by Warner Home Video

Cullen, B. (2000) *Why Golf? The Mystery of the Game Revisited*. NY: Simon and Schuster

Dodson, J. (1996) *Final Rounds*. NY: Bantam Books

Gately, I. (2001) *Tobacco*. London: Simon and Shuster

Ghose, A. (1963). *The future evolution of man; the divine life upon earth*. London: Allen & Unwin.

Grene, D. (Translator) (1987). *The history*. (Herodotus) Chicago: University of Chicago Press.

Haultain, A. (1986) *The Mystery of Golf*. Ailsa, Inc. (Original work published 1908)

LeGuin, U. (1998) *Lao Tzu: Tao Te Ching*. Boston: Shambala

Mascaro, J. (Translator) (1962) *The Bhagavad Gita*. NY: Penguin Books

Miller, L. (1996) *Beyond Golf*. Walpole, NH: Stillpoint Publishing

Murphy, M. (1972) *Golf In the Kingdom*. NY: Penguin Putnam Inc.

PGA AND USGA STEP TO NEW SETS OF TEES IN "Tee It Forward" Initiative (n.d.). Retrieved April 25, 2015, from http://www.pga.com/pga-and-usga-step-new-sets-tees-in-nationwide-tee-it-forward-initiative

PERFORMANCE OF THE AVERAGE MALE AMATEUR GOLFER. (n.d.). Retrieved April 25, 2015, from http://blog.trackmangolf.com/performance-of-the-average-male-amateur/

Pressfield, S. (1995) *The Legend of Bagger Vance*. NY: William Morrow and Co., Inc.

Ragonnet, J. (2007) Golf's Three Noble Truths. Novato, CA: New World Library

Rider-Waite tarot deck. (n.d.). Retrieved May 5, 2015, from http://en.wikipedia.org/wiki/Rider-Waite_tarot_deck

Rosen, S. (2000) *Gita on the Greens; the Mystical Tradition Behind Bagger Vance*. NY: Continuum

Smith, P. (2006, February 28). Who Invented Golf? China Takes a Swing. *The New York Times*. Retrieved from http://www.nytimes.com/2006/02/28/sports/28iht-chinagolf.html?pagewanted=all&_r=0

Updike, J. (1996) *Golf Dreams*. New York: Alfred A. Knopf

Wade, D. (2006) *Golf and the Art of War*. New York: Thunder's Mouth Press

Wible, A. (Editor) (2010) *Golf and Philosophy: Lessons from the Links*. Lexington, KY: The University Press of Kentucky

Made in the USA
Charleston, SC
25 May 2015